SPORTS GAMES

Video games and sports are the perfect match. They are both about having fun, friendly competition and mastering skills through practice. Those similarities show why game series like *Madden NFL* and *FIFA* are some of the biggest in the world.

Of course, video games do more than mirror the fun we get from playing our favorite sports in real life. Not everyone ends up playing in the NBA, winning a gold medal at the Olympics, or competing in the World Cup final. Video games allow us to fulfill the fantasy of playing for our favorite team, crossing the finish line in first place, or winning a Super Bowl trophy.

In this book, we will help you live out your athletic dreams by covering the biggest, best, and weirdest sports games out there, and giving you the expert tips and tricks you need to master them. Good luck, and go for the goal!

CONTENTS

FEATURES

04

THE BIGGEST GAMES

20

24

CONTENTS

26

40

54

46   Bluntslide

EDITOR IN CHIEF
Jon White

EDITOR
Stephen Ashby

SENIOR STAFF WRITER
Paul Walker-Emig

LEAD DESIGNER
Greg Whitaker

DESIGNER
Adam Markiewicz

PRODUCTION
Sanne de Boer, Fiona Hudson

COVER IMAGES

Rocket League © 2016 Psyonix, Inc. All Rights Reserved.

Madden 17 image used with permission of Electronic Arts Inc.

Steep © 2016 Ubisoft Entertainment. All Rights Reserved.

All titles, content, publisher names, trademarks, artwork, and associated imagery are trademarks and/or copyright material of their respective owners. All rights reserved.

ISBN 978-1-338-11055-5
10 9 8 7 6 5 4 3 2 1   17 18 19 20 21
Printed in the U.S.A.   40
First printing, April 2017

27 MASSIVE SPORTING MOMENTS

YOU'RE THE BEST AROUND

Sports games are all about big moments. The risky power slide around a muddy corner that increases your lead over second place. The spiraling ball thrown downfield in the final play of the game. The goal you score when you collect the ball just outside the box and rifle it into the net. After the sweat and the struggle in the heat of competition, it's those big moments that stay with us after the match is done and the glory starts to fade. These are the biggest moments from sports games, which cover everything from reversing Brock Lesnar's devastating finishing move, to dealing with flaming battleships on a golf course!

THE INTRODUCTION OF ULTIMATE TEAM

01 In 2008, EA Sports changed sports games forever. EA decided to release an experimental new feature to *FIFA 09*

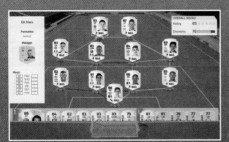

called Ultimate Team. This feature saw players opening packs of player cards to build the starting 11 of their choice, with the best players in the world being much rarer and therefore harder to find. It was an instant hit and Ultimate Team has since become the crowning jewel of the *FIFA* series, as other sports games looked at their own modes and tried to add new extras and features. For the first time, Ultimate Team proved there was more to sports video games than the action on the field—you'll now find it in *Madden* and *NHL*, too.

HITTING A HOME RUN

02 It's an obvious high point but crushing a home run out of the stadium in *MLB: The Show* feels good for all the right reasons. The sound of the bat striking the ball, the roar of the crowd, the celebration jog around the bases; these bring the experience to life.

MOTION CONTROLS MEET SPORTS

03 Xbox One continued what the Wii started, with its motion-detecting Kinect peripheral. With *Kinect Sports Rivals*, you can mimic the actions found in sports like rock climbing, jet ski racing, and soccer. It's tiring but fun!

TENNIS GETS THE NINTENDO TREATMENT

04 *Mario Tennis Open* adds some eccentric Nintendo-style mini-games. You have to collect star pieces, have Piranha Plants blind you with ink, and relive classic Mario levels.

RACING THROUGH THE STREETS OF MONACO

05 The tight streets of Monaco make for the most exciting race on the F1 calendar and you can relive it through *F1 2016*. Conquer Monaco and you can conquer anything.

MASTERING THE TOUGHEST FEAT IN SPORTS

06 There are no shortcuts in *Football Manager 2017*, so taking a non-league team to the Champions League is an impressive feat. It might be one of the hardest challenges in *any* sports game.

FLYING DOWN A MOUNTAIN AT EYE-WATERING SPEED

07 Ubisoft's *Steep* puts you up close and personal with a mountain. Whether you're skiing, flying, or paragliding, your heart will be racing!

WINNING ON A HAIL MARY PLAY

08 You're down three points in your *Madden NFL* game. You're 60 yards away from the end zone. There are seconds left on the clock. You have time for one more play. Everything is set up for the famous Hail Mary call, where the receivers run in a straight line down the field and you lob the ball high into the air toward them. It's a play that has a low chance of success, which is why it's rarely seen outside of the last, desperate few seconds in a game. But if you grab victory from the jaws of defeat, few moments in sports feel better.

MCILROY VS BATTLESHIP

09 EA found the perfect way to spice up golf in *Rory McIlroy PGA Tour*—a flaming battleship crashing onto the course! You actually have to strike the ball over the battleship itself.

SURVIVING AN ENTIRE RALLY STAGE

10 It's the ultimate test of skill and nerve. With rocks, mud, debris, trees, and other dangers lurking around, your focus needs to be locked in to survive an entire rally stage in *WRC5*.

CARVING UP A MOTOCROSS TRACK

11 You can *literally* carve up the muddy tracks in *MXGP 2*. Your bike reacts to the valleys that form in the mud across each turn, making it the bounciest racing game you'll ever play.

SKATEBOARDING'S TOUGHEST MOVE: THE 900

12 Tony Hawk was the first to land iconic trick The 900 and now you can re-create it. Not only can you do The 900 in *Tony Hawk's Pro Skater 5*, but you can even use it as part of a trick combo to earn massive point scores.

CONTROL REALITY

SCORING A GOAL FROM A DISTANCE

13 *PES 2017* demands a lot from its players who want to score from outside the box. You need the right power, right position, and even the right player. But when the ball hits the back of the net, it's a real high-five moment.

SCORING A LAST-SECOND WINNER

14 *Rocket League* is famous for its relentless quick-fire play, as the cars acrobatically flip and chase after the ball to smash it toward the opponent's goal. Because the arena is so small and you can quickly rocket up the field, you can switch from defense to attack in the blink of an eye. That means there's lots of potential to steal matches with last-second winners, as you

shore up an opponent's attack and race down the field to score a goal. It's clumsy, it's chaotic, it's carnage, and it's a lot of fun. Just remember—the final buzzer doesn't sound until the ball hits the floor!

REVERSING A FINISHER

16 Each bruising encounter in *WWE 2K17* ends with a deadly finisher, such as Brock Lesnar's "F5" or John Cena's "Attitude Adjustment." But if you get the timing just right—and your timing needs to be perfect—you can reverse the finisher, allowing the match to continue in dramatic fashion.

POTTING FROM DISTANCE

15 It's a shot you know you *shouldn't* take on. Almost every game of *Pure Pool* will have at least one long-distance shot, tempting you with its high-risk, high-reward payout.

MAKING THE BATTER SWEAT

17 Despite its simple arcade look, *Super Mega Baseball* offers a deep simulation of baseball, right down to the curve you can throw on pitches. Throw enough strikes and you will see the batter start to sweat with nerves and fear!

DON BRADMAN PROVING NICHE SPORTS ARE COOL

18 It might not be as popular as soccer or football, but *Don Bradman Cricket* proves that niche sports work just as well as video games. The strategic battle between batter and bowler is something baseball fans will definitely enjoy. You just might discover your new hobby!

NAILING THE PERFECT POWERSLIDE

19 Every vehicle in *DiRT Rally* feels like a hulking beast trapped in the claustrophobic confines of a car. Channeling the raw power of these machines into perfect powerslides around corners is an exhibition of your total dominance over those powerful cars.

HITTING A 3-POINTER

20 You'd think landing a thunderous slam dunk is the highlight of playing *NBA 2K17*. But think again. Just like how today's NBA is trending toward shooting from a distance, hitting a virtual 3-pointer is a real victory. It touches on everything that makes the game great: well-drilled teamwork to create an open shot; perfect timing to release the shot at the top of your jump to hear the swish of the net when it goes in.

Fakie Ollie

PLAYING QUICK BURSTS OF SPORTING FUN

21 Playing sports games doesn't mean you have to get involved in matches that are 15 minutes long. *OlliOlli* proves short blasts of 2-D skateboarding are fun—the levels are barely a minute long, but will keep you coming back to beat your own scores. It's tough to master, but incredibly rewarding to play.

THE BIGGEST SPORTS GAME EVER GETS UPGRADED

22 With over 82 million sales, *Wii Sports* is the biggest sports game of all time. *Wii Sports Club* is the HD Remaster of that game and also added online multiplayer, making it the definitive edition of a massive game.

MARIO & SONIC REENACT THE RIO OLYMPICS

23 The Rio Olympics are over but you can relive them through the colorful adventures of Mario and Sonic. From boxing to freestyle swimming, all the Rio Olympics events are here and given a unique twist.

UNUSUAL CROSSOVER

24 *Rocket League* brings tiny cars and oversized balls together, for an odd crossover that will appeal to sports and racing fans alike.

MULTIPLAYER SMASH HIT

25 The online multiplayer for *Rocket League* was a huge success, proving there's online life in sports titles outside the likes of *FIFA*.

SIZE DOESN'T MATTER

26 With 15 million players, *Rocket League* has ushered in a new wave of small sports titles, proving size isn't everything in fun games.

FAST AND FURIOUS

27 The boost on your car rockets you around the arena and makes *Rocket League* one of the fastest sports games ever made.

STATS

34 Madden games in series.

82 average review score.

#1 selling game in US in its first month.

40 licensed songs on soundtrack.

MADDEN NFL 17

AND IT'S A TOUCHDOWN!

It's rugged, it's robust, and it's relentless. *Madden NFL* captures the raw physicality of football and some of the bone-crunching hits will make you squirm. It feels like a fight for survival and that's especially true for *Madden NFL 17*. Defenses have been toughened up, so defensive players shadow their man through every twist and turn they take.

You need pin-perfect passes or runs to get past the close attention of defensive players. Get it right and it doesn't matter how quiet you are when playing other games; touchdowns in *Madden* will make you leap off the couch and cheer. There are few things in gaming as satisfying as launching a spiraling ball down the field and pulling it in for a touchdown.

TIPS & TRICKS

EASY DEFENSE
For easy defense, be a guard. Closest to the quarterback, he can bring him down the easiest.

RUN OR THROW?
When playing against friends, alternate between running and throwing plays to test their skills.

TOP 5 FUN TEAMS

NEW ENGLAND PATRIOTS

1 The combo of Tom Brady at quarterback and Rob Gronkowski at tight end is a defense crusher, making for an easy one-two punch to rely on.

PITTSBURGH STEELERS

2 Steeler Le'Veon Bell is one of the best players in the league. He has great hands for catching and the scorching speed needed to leave the defense eating dirt.

TAMPA BAY BUCCANEERS

4 With Jameis Winston, Mike Evans, and Charlie Sims forming the core of the Buccaneers' offensive line, this team is young, fast, athletic, and lots of fun to play.

LA RAMS

3 Freshly relocated from St. Louis, the LA Rams have a grinding defense that wears down the opposition. Get the ball back and you can hand it to star running back Todd Gurley.

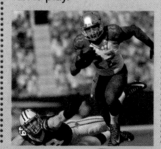

NEW ORLEANS SAINTS

5 Their defense won't stop many teams, but Drew Brees, Brandin Cooks, and Mark Ingram Jr. have the offensive power to outscore anyone.

OUT-OF-BOUNDS

You can run out-of-bounds with the ball. This stops the clock, giving you time to mount your comeback.

EXCITE-O-METER

Your journey to the Super Bowl starts here!

+ Easy to play, lots to master
+ Touchdowns are so satisfying
− Difficult game to learn

TIPS & TRICKS
MADDEN NFL 17

8 ESSENTIAL TIPS

PLAY TO YOUR TEAM'S STRENGTHS

01 Teams have the same strengths as they do in real life, so copy their real strategy. Focus on running the ball with the Bills, for example.

RUNNING IS SAFER

02 Remember that running is a safer option than throwing. You're less likely to make big gains, but you'll avoid risking interceptions or wasting downs with incomplete passes.

CHECK YOUR ROSTER

03 *Madden NFL* will update rosters in accordance to suspensions and injuries, which is realistic but weakens your team. Make sure you bring missing superstars back into your team.

QUICK TRICKS

KEEP PRACTICING
In Franchise mode, entering practice gives players a small stats boost in the next game.

RUN THE GAUNTLET
The Gauntlet is a fun mode that tests your skills. Use it to practice throwing, running, and defense.

WATCH THE SAFETY

04 Safeties are the players right at the back of the defense. Keep an eye on them when throwing. You want to avoid throwing to anyone drifting near safeties, as they'll try to grab the ball for an interception.

DIFFERENT PASSES

05 Use the left bumper and trigger to throw the ball high or low. Use high balls for long passes to receivers guarded by one man, low balls for passes in traffic.

PUMP FAKE

06 Flick the right analog stick with the quarterback for a pump fake, a pretend pass. This can confuse defensive players and give your receivers a chance to break free.

RUNNING QUARTERBACKS

07 Quarterbacks like Cam Newton or Russell Wilson can run with a ball. Keep an eye on the field when you have it and wait for gaps in the defense.

CLOCK MANAGEMENT

08 A great skill is clock management. If you're winning, run the ball more often to drain the clock. If you're behind, run out-of-bounds to stop the clock.

CHANGE THE CAMERA
In defense, press Up or Down on the D-pad to change the camera for a view of the opposing quarterback.

TAKING SLIDE
When running the ball, remember you can slide to end the play early. You'll avoid an injury or a fumble.

STATS

CRISTIANO RONALDO

is the highest-rated player, with an Overall stat of 94.

8 pro soccer players consulted on the game's story.

1ST *FIFA* game made in EA's Frostbite engine.

FROSTBITE 3

OVER **650** playable teams.

FIFA 17

LIVING THE DREAM

You expect amazingly realistic players, authentic stadiums, and great gameplay from every *FIFA* game, but this entry also has something brand new to offer. *FIFA 17* introduces a new story mode called The Journey where you take control of a promising youngster named Alex Hunter. It lets you live every soccer fan's dream as you rise up the ranks to become a legend for your favorite Premier League club. Your performances on the field and the decisions you make off it will determine how your story will progress. Added to the great modes the game already has, including Ultimate Team and Co-op Seasons, *FIFA 17* truly is a star on and off the field.

TIME LINE

A RISING STAR 1993
The game that started it all off was *FIFA International Soccer*, first released on the Sega Genesis.

THE ULTIMATE MODE 2008
FIFA 09 was the first to have Ultimate Team—as a download—which has now become a headline mode.

TOP 5 FIFA MINI-GAMES

FUT DRAFT SUMMARY

TOP PLAYERS

76 TEAM CHEMISTRY

Forwards **81** Midfielders **81** Defenders **79**

Spain
4 PLAYERS

ULTIMATE TEAM

1 The success of Ultimate Team has gone far beyond what EA could have expected. The card-collecting mini-game has grown so much over the years that it is now arguably *FIFA*'s flagship mode.

SKILL GAMES

3 Giving you a skill mini-game to play during loading times was a masterstroke. Sometimes, you'll even find yourself sticking with the skill game even when the match is ready to go!

CLASSIC MODE

4 *FIFA 06* had a classic mode that let you play the original *FIFA International Soccer* within the game. We'd love to see that retro mode return!

INDOOR SOCCER

2 *FIFA 97* and *FIFA 98* included a mode that let you play indoor soccer matches with small teams of five or six on a side. This great mode eventually spawned the *FIFA Street* series and we haven't seen it since.

FOOTII

5 *FIFA 09* on the Wii included an 8 vs. 8 mode called Footii, where you plated with Miis instead of the usual characters. By beating teams from around the world, you would unlock their superstars.

EXCITE-O-METER

Everything we love about *FIFA*, plus some new features!

+ New story mode
+ New set piece system
+ Managers appear for first time

MOVING FORWARD 2016
FIFA 17 proves EA isn't done trying new things with the introduction of its story-based The Journey mode.

TIPS & TRICKS
FIFA 17

8 ESSENTIAL TIPS

CHEMISTRY MATTERS

01 Don't just focus on player ratings when picking players in Ultimate Team. Getting a high chemistry rating by pairing up players of the same nationality or from the same team can be more effective.

HOT PROSPECTS

02 Try to grab some young players with high potential in Career Mode. While Anthony Martial, Kingsley Coman, and Daniele Rugani are all rated at 78, for example, they all have the potential to reach a rating of 86.

CORNER BALL!

03 Struggling to score from a corner kick? Try aiming for the front or back post areas of the field. Your players have a better chance of getting a decent run up here and can get a good angle on their headers.

DUMMY THROWS

04 You can perform dummy throws for the first time in *FIFA 17*. Press Square or Circle and then X on PlayStation, or X or B and then A on Xbox to dummy your throw.

TIPS & TRICKS

PROTECT THE BALL
Hold L2 to shield the ball from your opponent. This works best with strong players.

TRY THE DRILLS
FIFA 17's practice drills are worth playing. They introduce you to all the skills you can use on the field.

DRIVEN SHOTS

05 Build up your shooting power bar, then tap the shoot button again just as the player is about to strike the ball to perform a driven shot. This way, you'll put tons of power in your shots without them soaring over the bar.

A SPECIAL CARD!

06 If you finish *FIFA 17*'s The Journey mode, you will be rewarded with a *FIFA* Ultimate Team card of the character that stars in the mode, Alex Hunter.

THREADED BALL

08 To perform a threaded through ball that goes between the defensive players and deeper into space than a regular through ball, hold down RB or R1 when you press the through ball button.

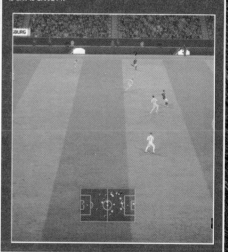

MIX UP CROSSES

07 Use different cross types depending on the situation. Pressing cross once will send the ball toward the far post, double tapping will send a lower cross to the near post, and triple tapping sends in a low cross.

PRACTICE PENS

The penalty system has changed, so practice to avoid missing crucial chances.

TACTICAL CHANGE

Try making some changes to your formation and tactics to change your fortunes.

TOP 10

WEIRD SPORTS GAMES

INAZUMA ELEVEN

You've got to explore your town to recruit and train players to improve your team in this title that blends soccer with RPG gameplay. On the field, you can use special moves to dodge past other players and pull off spectacular shots.

PUSH ME PULL YOU

You control two heads connected by one wormlike body in this crazy game where you have to wrestle control of a ball onto your side of the arena to win. Things get even more confusing in two-player, with each player controlling one head of the body.

> **"YOU HAVE TO WRESTLE CONTROL OF A BALL ONTO YOUR SIDE OF THE ARENA."**

QWOP

In this hilarious running game, you have to control your athlete's thighs and calves individually. It's incredibly fiddly, so you clumsily wobble to the finish line. That's the whole point, though—*QWOP* is meant to be a silly game that makes you laugh.

#IDARB

Imagine a cross between *Super Mario* and handball, and you're getting close to understanding this platform sports game. Your objective is to throw the ball into the opponent's goal. If you manage to bounce the ball off a few walls first, you'll get extra points. Of course, the other team will be leaping around trying to stop you, so prepare for chaos!

"GANG BEASTS OFFERS ITS OWN VERSION OF WRESTLING."

GANG BEASTS

Gang Beasts offers up its own version of the kind of wrestling action you would see in a Royal Rumble. It does have a level where you have to throw your opponents over the top rope, but it's also got levels set in a sausage factory, on a Ferris wheel, and a whole lot more.

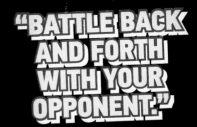

NIDHOGG

If you ever thought fencing wasn't exciting enough, then maybe *Nidhogg* will make you think again. Battle back and forth with your opponent in an exciting game of skill to push them through a series of screens. Finish them and your reward, for some reason, is to be eaten by a giant flying worm!

"BATTLE BACK AND FORTH WITH YOUR OPPONENT."

MONKEY TENNIS

Super Monkey Ball 2 had a number of cool party mini-games in it, including Monkey Shot and Monkey Soccer. The best of the bunch, though, is Monkey Tennis, where you play Tennis as a monkey rolling around inside a giant ball.

SUPER POLE RIDERS

Part of the Sportsfriends package of games, *Super Pole Riders* is a weird version of pole vaulting. Instead of trying to vault over a bar, you use your pole to vault toward a ball hanging on a rope that you need to push to your opponent's side of the field to score a point.

BLITZBALL

No one came into *Final Fantasy X* or *X-2* thinking they'd spend hours playing an underwater turn-based sports mini-game and scouring the world for new players to improve their team. However, that's exactly what happened when they encountered the fictional sport of Blitzball.

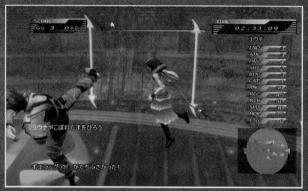

"YOUR GOAL IS TO SMASH A GOLF BALL AROUND A ROOM!"

DANGEROUS GOLF

One of the great things about video games is that they let you do things you can't do in real life. This is the case in *Dangerous Golf*, where your goal is to smash a golf ball around in a room to damage as many glasses, bits of furniture, and other valuables as you can.

ROCKET LEAGUE

ROCKET LEAGUE

ONE MORE MATCH ...

The new modes keep on coming in *Rocket League*. We've had an ice hockey–style mode called Snow Day, the basketball-inspired Hoops mode, and a Rumble mode that introduces crazy power-ups that let you harpoon the ball, kick your opponents out of the way with a boot on a spring, and a whole lot more. The commitment to new challenges is part of *Rocket League*'s long-lasting appeal, but the main reason people keep playing it is because the game is so good. *Rocket League*'s perfectly balanced version of soccer, with rocket-powered cars, has all the excitement, drama, and intensity you get from a real sport. The new modes are great, but every match of the standard game is so different that you won't need an extra reason to keep coming back.

TIPS & TRICKS

HOOP MASTER
In Hoops mode, you can fly up through the hoop to stop opposition goals.

HANG BACK
Your whole team shouldn't go for the same ball. Hang back when others are in a position to get to it.

TOP 5 RUMBLE POWER-UPS

MAGNETIZER

1 The Magnetizer attracts the ball to your car. Fly through the air toward the goal, and you can take the ball out of your opponent's reach and score for your team in the process!

PLUNGER

2 This power-up lets you grab onto the ball with a plunger on a cord. Pulling a ball off the line to save a goal with it feels great!

DISRUPTOR

3 This power-up is great for messing with players on the other team. It forces them to drive uncontrollably, sending them weaving all over the place. It'll buy you a few seconds, too!

SPIKE

5 Drive into the ball with this power-up and it will stick to your car. Now you've just got to weave your way around your opponents to try to get to the goal.

SWAPPER

4 Use the Swapper to switch places with an opponent. This helps both offense and defense. Try switching with a goalkeeper.

EXCITE-O-METER

Awesome rocket-powered sport that keeps on giving.

+ Every match is new
+ New modes always being added
+ Most DLC is free

COORDINATE KICKOFF

Usually, the person closest to the ball should go for it at kickoff. Use in-game quick chat to let the other players know.

NBA 2K17

THE MVP OF SPORTS GAMES

Running a pick and roll at the top of the key, blowing past a screen, and finishing with a Euro Step layup. Sounds confusing but this strange language will make perfect sense to you as an *NBA 2K17* player, the most in-depth sports simulator ever made. You'll begin with the passing and shooting basics, with the excitable commentary and gorgeous graphics making you feel as though you're in an actual sports broadcast. But as you invest more time into *NBA 2K17*, you'll see the depth that lurks beyond its shiny surface. You can master advanced basketball plays, set coaching strategies, and pull off moves that would make James Harden nod with approval. You can even become the general manager of an NBA team, build or create your own courts, and design team logos.

TIPS & TRICKS

SHOT TIMING
Release your shot at the peak of your jump to increase accuracy. You can pass out of your shot, too.

DON'T ALWAYS SPRINT
When defending, try jogging around the court rather than sprinting, to conserve your energy.

TOP 5 SUPERSTARS TO TRY

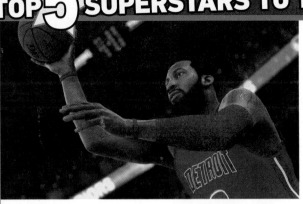

ANDRE DRUMMOND

1 Detroit's powerful center led the league in rebounds last year. Drummond's athleticism makes him a great choice in *NBA 2K17* if you want to grab your teammates' missed shots.

KARL-ANTHONY TOWNS

2 Even at seven feet tall, Towns has the dribbling and shooting skills of a nimble point guard.

DRAYMOND GREEN

3 If you like harassing players on defense and hitting shots, use Draymond Green. He's quick, strong, and big, so he can defend every position!

KEVIN DURANT

5 Durant was already one of the best players in the league, and now that he's on the Warriors, he's even better because the defense can't focus solely on him.

JIMMY BUTLER

4 Chicago's scoring machine can muscle past guards to drive to the hoop and hit jump shots at a distance. To score in a variety of ways, pick Butler.

LAYUPS NOT DUNKS

Dunks are flashy and fun but not effective if there are defensive players in the way. Go for a safer layup instead.

EXCITE-O-METER

The most realistic sports game ever made.

+ Teaches the sport
+ Looks like a TV broadcast
− Difficult to learn

TIPS & TRICKS
NBA 2K17

POST UP

02 If you can't create a good shot, and you have a strong center on your team, pass the ball to your center and hold the left trigger to post up. This will put your back to the basket, allowing you to get close for a scoring opportunity.

TAKE YOUR TIME
01 When you have the ball, you have 24 seconds to take a shot. Make the most of this time. Pass the ball around if there are no openings, while looking for defensive players who are struggling to keep up with the play.

TRANSITION POINTS
03 Whenever you get a steal, block, or defensive rebound, look to pass the ball up the court immediately. If one of your teammates is breaking away, it's an easy scoring opportunity before the defending team can get back to the basket.

TIGHT DEFENSE
04 Holding the left trigger will activate intense defense, which keeps a player poised for shot or pass attempts. It decreases an opponent's chance of making shots.

TIPS & TRICKS

BEGINNER TEAM
First time? Use the Golden State Warriors. They shoot well and have great defense.

LEARN SHOT STICK
Pull off hops or shot attempts with the right analog stick. Try it in the practice court!

STEP THROUGH

05 Tapping the right stick causes a pump fake, where you pretend to shoot. Holding the right stick during the pump fake leads to a step through, turning the faked attempt into an actual shot. Use this move when close to the basket.

BOUNCE PASS

06 If you're worried about a pass being intercepted, try using a bounce pass. This makes it harder for opponents to steal the pass but it also slows the pass down, so don't use this pass when you need to be quick.

HUMAN DEFENSE

08 Human players are much looser than the computer at defense, so you can get away with risky play. Try driving the ball to the hoop more often.

CHECK 3-POINT RATINGS

07 Check your team's ratings to find your strongest 3-point shooter. If you're behind, start taking shots with your 3-point shooter to try to close the gap.

CHECK FATIGUE

Watch the fatigue of both teams at the end, and give fresher players more time.

DON'T GET FRUSTRATED

It's hard to keep track of all the moves to learn. First learn the basics and keep practicing!

TOP 7 eSPORTS GAMES

DOTA 2

DOTA 2 is regularly in the top three most-watched games online. What makes it really big, though, is that teams of pro gamers compete to win millions of dollars in prize money at the International competition every year.

STREET FIGHTER V

The battle of wits between two *Street Fighter* players trying to predict what their opponent will do next is as entertaining to watch as an eSport as it is to play!

HALO 5: GUARDIANS

Multiplayer has long been one of the biggest strengths of the *Halo* series, so it's no surprise that this awesome FPS has become a big player in the eSports scene.

WORLD OF TANKS

Don't let the fact that it's got tanks in it fool you—*World of Tanks* is more about cautious strategy and patience than it is about big explosions. That makes this team-based tank game perfect for eSports. It's free to play, so why not try it yourself? You've got nothing to lose.

SUPER SMASH BROS.

The simplicity of *Super Smash Bros.* makes it a great starting point for a beginner looking to have some fun with fighting games or looking to check out some eSports. Plus, it has all of Nintendo's greatest characters in one game!

HEROES OF THE STORM

A relatively new player on the eSports scene, this MOBA that features characters from *World of Warcraft*, *StarCraft*, and *Overwatch* is growing fast.

OVERWATCH

This awesome team-based shooter where you have to work together with your teammates to get the most out of your characters' abilities was built with eSports in mind.

STATS

156 wrestlers on the roster.

Goldberg **12 years** appears after absent from WWE.

12 personality traits define each wrestler.

4TH 🎮 WWE game made by 2K.

WWE 2K17

CHAMPION OF THE WORLD

With over 150 wrestlers, a huge creation suite where you can make your own Superstars, and a Universe mode where you can take control of shows and storylines, *WWE 2K17* is packed with possibilities. Speaking of possibilities, *WWE 2K17* adds some new ones. You can now have promo battles with your opponents, just like on TV, picking what you want to say to make the crowd cheer or boo you. Backstage brawls also make a return to the series, letting you use the environment, and anything you find lying around in it, to weaken your opponent. Whether you want to take a created wrestler to the top in career mode, play against your friends in crazy four-way ladder matches, or manage the roster in Universe mode, *WWE 2K17* has everything a wrestling fan could want.

TIPS AND TRICKS

MANAGE YOUR STAMINA
Watch your stamina while you're attacking. You could become vulnerable.

PRACTICE REVERSALS
Timing of reversals needs to be right. Practice them in exhibition matches.

TOP 5 WWE ALTERNATIVES

GANG BEASTS

1 This funny brawling game frequently has you wrestling opponents to try to lift them above your head and even has a level set in a wrestling ring.

SUPER SMASH BROS.

2 Do you want more of the chaos that *WWE 2K17* offers in multi-person events such as ladder matches? *Super Smash Bros.* can give you that, along with some of your favorite gaming characters.

FIRE PRO WRESTLING

3 The *Fire Pro Wrestling* series is known for its more complex and technically challenging take on wrestling, so it might be for you if you want more depth.

STREET FIGHTER V

4 If *WWE 2K17* has given you a taste for competition, *Street Fighter V* is the next step. Characters Alex, Zangief, and R. Mika have wrestling moves of their own.

WWF NO MERCY

5 If you don't mind going retro, then *WWF No Mercy* has a reputation as one of the best wrestling games ever, even all these years after its 2000 release.

MIX IT UP

To improve the rating of your matches, make sure you vary your offense. Repeating the same moves just won't do it.

EXCITE-O-METER

Gives wrestling fans everything they want.

+ Authentic entrances
+ Option to customize
— Core gameplay hasn't changed

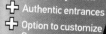

STATS

5 ways to explore.

3 Play with other players.

21 Drop Zones to find on Mont Blanc.

15,776 ft highest summit in the game.

STEEP

A SLIPPERY SLOPE TO FUN

A whole mountain range is your playground in *Steep*, and this awesome open world can be explored in four different ways. Skiing, snowboarding, wing suit flying, and paragliding are your options for getting around, as well as for taking part in races and events. While you can play on your own, it is also possible to hook up with friends to explore the world together, race against one another, or compete to see who can pull off the coolest stunts. Being able to discover new challenges, snowboard with your friends, or just enjoy the scenery, gives the game a real sense of freedom. It also has some really cool features, like saving replays of your awesome stunts (or epic crashes) and setting challenges for your friends to take on.

TIME LINE

THE SIM STUDIO 1996
Developer Ubisoft Annecy is founded in France and focuses on simulation games in the early part of its life.

MULTIPLAYER MOVE 2010
Focus turns to multiplayer, working on multiplayer modes for a number of Ubisoft games.

TONY HAWK'S PRO SKATER 3

1 This third entry added the ability to pull off reverts, allowing you to add tricks performed on half-pipes into your combos.

TRACKMANIA TURBO

2 Racing has never been more extreme than in *Trackmania Turbo*. With mind-blowing tracks filled with loops, jumps, and tight turns, it's a real challenge to try to beat the high scores.

SSX TRICKY

3 Soar through the sky performing amazing tricks you would never see in real life in this crazy snowboarding title. The focus is on fun rather than realism.

TRIALS FUSION

4 Trying to get to the end of a track in *Trials Fusion* can be hard enough. Once you master it, though, it's great fun trying to beat your friends' scores.

SKATE 3

5 The *Skate* series more realistic approach to skateboarding made it a real favorite for fans who didn't like the *Tony Hawk's* series wackier take on the sport.

INSPIRATION 2013 Development of *Steep* begins, inspired by the studio's location close to the Alps.

EXCITE-O-METER

Great fun to explore with your friends.

➕ Freedom of play
➕ Can share replays
➕ Custom challenges

TOP 10

MOBILE SPORTS GAMES

NEW STAR SOCCER

New Star Soccer is a perfect blend of on-the-field action and off-the-field decision-making. Matches play out as a series of key moments where you use touch screen controls to set the direction and spin of the ball to curl it around opposition players. Off the field, you can improve your stats, win over fans, and must make crucial decisions about your player's career.

FOOTBALL HEROES PRO 2016

Crazy special moves that give you super bursts of speed, or that let you leap over tacklers, make this a fun and cartoony version of the real sport. There is some realism, too, though, with over 1,800 true NFL players to play with.

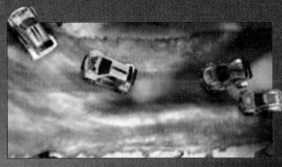

DRAWRACE 2

Before each race starts, you have to quickly draw a line around the track on your touch screen. Your car will then do its best to follow it. Draw the line too quickly, or get the cornering wrong, and your car might spin out of control. Get it right, though, and it feels great!

SUPER STICKMAN GOLF 3

Trying to get your ball past buzzsaws, over giant trees, and through tiny gaps to the hole in *Super Stickman Golf 3* is a lot of fun. That's before you start using the cool new power-ups and master the ability to add spin to the ball.

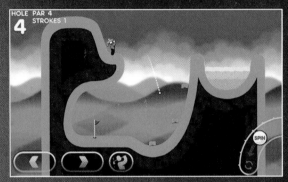

FOOTBALL MANAGER MOBILE 2016

The greatest soccer management series of all time lets you take charge of your favorite team and do whatever you can to lead them to glory. Choose your tactics, buy and sell players, and tweak your strategies to get the best of your opposition to lead your team to trophies.

"GET THE BEST OF YOUR OPPOSITION."

NBA JAM BY EA SPORTS

NBA Jam was a huge hit in the 1990s. This updated mobile version brings the classic two-on-two arcade style gameplay to mobile devices, complete with ridiculous slam dunks, big head mode, and flaming basketballs.

TABLE TENNIS TOUCH

The touch controls work perfectly in this amazing table tennis game where you guide your floating paddle with swipes of your finger to determine the power, direction, and spin of the ball. The game can be played single-player, but also has a multiplayer mode.

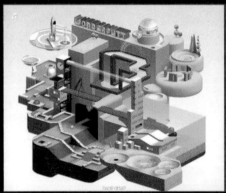

WONDERPUTT

In this beautiful golf game, the level changes around you as you play, with alien abductions, cows, ski slopes, and torpedoes all making an appearance! It's a great game to play in short bursts and will keep you coming back as you try to improve on your best score.

"YOU TAKE CONTROL OF ALL ASPECTS OF THE GAME, FROM PITCHING TO BATTING."

MLB PERFECT INNING 16

Essential for any baseball fan out there is *MLB Perfect Inning 16*. You take control of all aspects of the game, from pitching to batting, using controls built specifically for touch screen, and can guide your chosen team to glory in the game's Season Mode.

RECKLESS RACING 3

Anyone who has played a racing game knows how satisfying it can be to perfectly drift around a corner. That's what makes *Reckless Racing 3* so great: It's built for you to skid around every corner in the game. Once you get the hang of the controls, it feels amazing.

STATS

18 events to play.

Up to **FOUR** players.

34 characters.

Sonic is the fastest character with a speed rating of **9**

MARIO & SONIC AT THE RIO 2016 OLYMPIC GAMES

GOING FOR GOLD

There are so many different sports for you to try in this bright and joyful version of the Olympics. There is archery, beach volleyball, boxing, javelin, gymnastics, and rugby, to name just a few that you can choose from! Some of the events even have their own special Duel version that includes power-ups from the *Mario* and *Sonic* series to shake things up.

Trying out all the different events is great fun, especially when you play with friends to see who can win a medal in each sport. We also love the fact that the game is full of cool characters from the *Mario* and *Sonic* games, like Wario, Bowser, Donkey Kong, Dr. Eggman, Tails, and more.

TIME LINE

ON YOUR MARKS! 2007
The first entry in the series was released to tie in with the 2008 Beijing Olympics.

CHILLING OUT 2009
Mario & Sonic at the Olympic Winter Games swapped track and field for skis and bobsleds.

TOP 5 EVENTS

1 RHYTHMIC GYMNASTICS

This plays out like rhythm action games. Buttons will come down in time to the music and you've got to hit them at the right time.

2 RUGBY SEVENS

The team-based nature of this sport is really fun and it is one of the deeper sports that are on offer in *Mario & Sonic at the Rio 2016 Olympic Games.*

4 EQUESTRIAN

Whether you enjoy nailing all the jumps perfectly, or just like laughing at Wario on a horse, this event is sure to make you smile.

3 DUEL VOLLEYBALL

Power-ups that allow you to throw red shells at your opponents, among other things, can give you much more to think about in this version of volleyball.

5 SOCCER

Scoring a goal is always satisfying in soccer games and that doesn't change in this game's take on the sport. Putting together a perfect series of passes that ends in a goal is a great feeling!

EVERYONE'S WELCOME 2016 *Mario & Sonic at the Rio 2016 Olympic Games* is the first to add new characters since 2009.

EXCITE-O-METER

A great game to play with friends.

+ Tons of events
− Some events are too easy
+ Awesome multiplayer

TIPS & TRICKS

MARIO & SONIC AT THE RIO 2016 OLYMPIC GAMES

8 ESSENTIAL TIPS

WATCH THOSE TACKLES

01 Don't slide tackle from behind when you are playing soccer. If you do, you're almost certain to commit a foul and give a free kick or penalty to the other team. Tackle from the front or side instead.

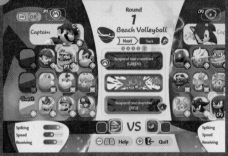

TRY NEW CHARACTERS

02 Every character in the game has different stats, so if you're struggling in an event with your favorite character, try switching to another one. Sonic's speed makes him great at the 100m, for example.

GET DIDDY KONG

03 New characters can be unlocked by completing certain tasks. For example, if you can defeat Diddy Kong in the 110m Hurdles on Day One of the Mario adventure, you will unlock him.

QUICK TRICKS

DREAM EVENTS
Collect power-ups when you can and beware of the enemy team trying to take you out.

GET FRIENDS INVOLVED
Get friends or family to join you in multiplayer for *Mario & Sonic at the Rio 2016 Olympic Games.*

BULL'S-EYE!

04 When you are playing the archery event, you can hold down A on the Wii U GamePad and the camera will zoom in to give you a closer view of the target you are aiming for.

DOUBLE YOUR REWARDS

05 A Lakitu appears on the beach after every five gold medals. Talk to it to receive 30 coins and 30 rings. If you dress your Mii in a full Lakitu costume, then you'll receive double the coins and rings!

UNLOCK TOURNAMENTS

06 The sand statue at the tournament gate will be completed after you win five single matches. This allows you to start taking part in tournaments.

GO SHOPPING

07 Completing tournaments will unlock item stands. You can then spend coins or rings at the stands to buy items. You never know what you're going to see at the stand, so keep your fingers crossed that there will be something new.

DRESS FOR SUCCESS

08 If you choose to play as a Mii, your character's base stats will be low. By dressing them up, you can improve your Mii's speed, power, and technique.

TALK TO EVERYONE

Talk to every character you can see. This will often unlock new items, such as countries' flags.

CARNIVAL TIME

After winning the level one tournaments, Mario, Bowser, and other carnival floats will appear.

NHL 17

STATS

26TH mainline entry in the *NHL* series.

VLADIMIR TARASENKO won the cover vote against **8** other players.

All **27** ECHL teams make their debut.

Sidney Crosby is the highest rated HUT player at **95**.

NHL 17 ICE COOL

EA SPORTS NHL

HONDA
The Power of Dreams

The action on the ice is as intense and exciting as it has ever been in *NHL 17*. A few new tweaks such as improved goalies and a net battle feature only makes things better. Where *NHL 17* really improves over the last couple of entries, though, is in the variety of modes on offer. You can create a star-packed team in Draft Champions, compete for your country in the World Cup of Hockey, manage a team and make all the key decisions in Franchise Mode, collect your favorite players in Hockey Ultimate Team, live career-defining moments in Be a Pro, and create your own custom arena in Arena Creator. With amazing authenticity, great customization options, and so many ways to experience the sport, fans of ice hockey are sure to be satisfied.

TIPS & TRICKS

BREAKAWAY SCORE
The pullback wrister is a great way to score if you've got time on a breakaway.

SURPRISE SHOT
Hold up during a face-off to take a quick shot. It might surprise a goalie now and again.

TOP 5 MOMENTS

DRAFT CHAMPIONS

1 In this mode, you go through a series of rounds where you make tough choices about which players and hockey legends to draft into your team before taking them on the ice to compete.

FRANCHISE MODE

2 Take control of your favorite team and make key decisions on everything from ticket prices to marketing.

HOCKEY ULTIMATE TEAM

3 Just like the Ultimate Team modes in *Madden* and *FIFA*, *NHL 17*'s own version lets you build up a team of players by buying virtual packs of cards.

ARENA CREATOR

5 It's probably not going to be a mode you drop into a lot, but being able to make your own arena, customizing the ice surface and the goal songs, for example, is really cool.

WORLD CUP OF HOCKEY

4 For the first time since *NHL 2005*, you can choose an international team and compete in the World Cup, with all the official teams, players, and uniforms.

EXCITE-O-METER

Exciting action on the ice and lots to do off it.

+ Improved goalies
+ ECHL teams have been introduced
− Little HUT changes

SYNERGIZE
In Ultimate Team, you'll get a boost by matching synergies with your play style.

STATS

250 challenges to complete.

5 worlds to play through.

OlliOlli 2 has an extra **9,000 frames** of hand-drawn animation.

Up to four-player splitscreen.

OLLIOLLI2: WELCOME TO OLLIWOOD

SKATING AFTER HIGH SCORES

Whether you're playing the original *OlliOlli*, or its awesome sequel, *OlliOlli2: Welcome to Olliwood*, the goal is the same: Skate to the end of the stage and score as many points as you can on the way. To do this, you've got to pull off epic tricks, flicks, grabs, and spins as you leap, manual, and grind your way through the stage. You might be satisfied with finishing a level at first, but you'll soon find that the fun in *OlliOlli* is in returning to levels to try to complete them in one combo and push your score higher. With crazy levels that see you grinding on roller-coaster rails, jumping off firework-loaded ramps, and skating on TNT-carrying trains in the Wild West, *OlliOlli* is as fun to look at as it is to play.

TIME LINE

PUSHING OFF 2014
The original *OlliOlli* hits PlayStation Vita first in January 2014.

SKATING TO SUCCESS 2015
OlliOlli 2 builds on features from the first game, adding split-level routes and much more.

TOP 5 HIGH SCORE TIPS

GRIND SWITCHING

1 In *OlliOlli2*, you can switch to another grind while you are already grinding a rail. Sneaking in two grinds on a rail using this method is a real help for your score.

x4   Feeble Grind   3K+

LEARN THE LEVEL

x19   Bluntslide   150K+

2 Don't worry about getting a high score on your first run through a level. You need to play through it a few times so that you know what is coming up next.

KEEP SPINNING

3 Spinning in the air pushes up your score multiplier, which is very important when you're trying to move up the leaderboard.

VARIETY

5 If you repeat the same tricks over and over, you will get fewer points. Try to mix up your tricks instead to maximize your score.

PERFECTION

4 Master the timing of landings to make sure you don't get "Sloppy" landings that push your score down. Practice until you get "Perfects."

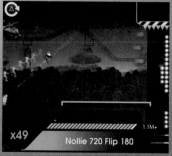

x49   Nollie 720 Flip 180   1.1M+

Switch BS Revert >> Nose Manu   471K+

THE COMPLETE PACKAGE 2016 *OlliOlli: Epic Combo Edition* is released, including both *OlliOlli* and *OlliOlli2*, videos, interviews, and *OlliOlli2*'s soundtrack.

EXCITE-O-METER

An amazing score attack game that keeps you coming back.

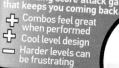

+ Combos feel great when performed
+ Cool level design
− Harder levels can be frustrating

BEHIND THE SCENES
OLLIOLLI

ROLL7 CO-FOUNDER SIMON BENNETT TELLS US ABOUT THE MAKING OF THE STUDIO'S AMAZING SKATING SERIES

x4 • Feeble Grind • 3K+

Where did the idea for *OlliOlli* come from?

John, our creative director, and I are skateboarders. He had been playing with a bunch of ideas while we were working on client projects. He made a little prototype in 2-D that was all about timing to land your jumps. It was a super-addictive game on mobile, then we approached PlayStation and they asked us to build it for PlayStation Vita.

How did you go about coming up with ideas for and designing the crazy themes for each level?

It was a lot of back and forth as to where we would set the levels, but we opted for five locations around the world. John then set about making levels with obstacles and art assets. We picked cultural elements from each place and focused on a color scheme that matched.

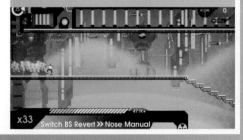

x33 • Switch BS Revert » Nose Manual • 471K+

How did you go about animating tricks? Did you have to get a skateboarder in to help with this?

John used lots of slow-mo videos of pros skating as reference (as well as his own knowledge of tricks). We had a lot of fun doing tricks in the office and tweaking the pixel art. Unlike 3-D animation, every frame of the trick was painstakingly hand-drawn; there are tens of thousands of frames in that little skater!

"EVERY FRAME WAS PAINSTAKINGLY HAND-DRAWN!"

Have you been surprised by the success of *OlliOlli*?

Definitely—we didn't expect it to go so big! Winning a BAFTA was a real highlight. It has given the studio the ability to make more games. We did *OlliOlli2: Welcome to Olliwood* and *NOT A HERO* the next year, and we are now working on a much bigger 3-D game.

How difficult was it to make the games being a small team?

Really tough, actually, especially considering it was our first big game, but you learn as you go! We had a tiny team and people had to jump onto loads of tasks. Most studios making triple-A games are about 400 people. The *OlliOlli* team was about eight.

How good are you and the team at the game? Do you have any impressive high scores on the leaderboards?

Well, Sam, our QA lead on the project, has two Guinness World Records for *OlliOlli* — so pretty good, I guess!

GAMER CHALLENGE

CHECK YOUR GAMING CRED

01 Which *FIFA* game first introduced Ultimate Team?

02 In which golf game is there a battleship on the course?

03 Which game has an eSport event called the International?

04 True or false: *OlliOlli2* has levels where you grind on roller-coaster rails.

05 Are there 5, 11, or 30 power-ups in total in *Rocket League*'s Rumble mode?

06 Who is the cover star of *NHL 17*?

07 Which team has Tom Brady at quarterback in *Madden NFL 17*?

08 *QWOP* is a game based on which sport?

09 How do you control your car in *DrawRace 2*?

10 Which basketball game has a big head mode?

11 Are there 26, 98, or 156 wrestlers in total on *WWE 2K17*'s roster?

12 How many extreme sports are there in *Steep*?

13 In which city is the 2016 version of *Mario & Sonic at the Olympics* set?

14 Which racing game re-creates a famous track in Monaco?

15 Which skateboarder is famous for performing The 900?

16 How many Euro league teams are in *NBA 2K17*?

HOW DID YOU SCORE?

 0–5 **Gaming noob:** you need to step it up!

 6–10 **Casual Gamer:** you could do better!

 11–15 **Hardcore Gamer:** you really know your stuff!

 16 **Gaming God:** you totally rock!

WINDJAMMERS

FRISBEE HAS NEVER BEEN SO MUCH FUN!

FIRST RELEASED
April 8, 1994

DEVELOPER
Data East

Originally released in the arcades before coming out on the Neo Geo, *Windjammers* is a cool mix of tennis and Frisbee. The objective of the game is to throw your disk over the net and get it past your opponent and into their goal, or have it land on their side of the court. To do this you've got a number of skills to use: You can use a normal throw, toss the disk up high in the air, perform curving throws, and even special throws that are unique to each character. Every time a special throw is countered, it then gets sent back at a higher speed, creating some really intense rallies!

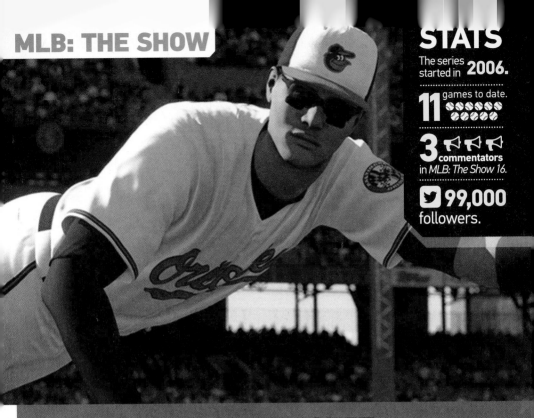

MLB: THE SHOW

PITCH PERFECT

It's the ultimate contest: pitcher vs. batter. The pitcher is trying to sneak the ball into the catcher's safe hands and the batter is hoping to crush the ball out of the stadium. Who will win? It's that thrilling head-to-head that makes baseball such fun to play. Whichever side of the match-up you're on, you have to consider how tired the players are, their confidence, their pitching and batting preferences, and more. That attention to detail is what has powered this series over the years and it seeps into every aspect of the game. There are individual fan signs for players, the commentators will talk about player's histories, and umpires even make the odd mistake, just like in real baseball. This game really is everything a baseball fan could ever wish for.

QUICK TRICKS

VARY PITCHES
Alternate between the types of pitches to keep the batter guessing at what's coming.

AIM FOR THE CORNERS
Aim for the edges of the box making it harder for the batter to hit the ball.

TOP 5 MODES

ROAD TO THE SHOW

1 You take a rookie from draft day to signing with his first team to becoming a superstar. You can also activate ShowTime in this mode, slowing down time when batting or fielding in critical situations.

FRANCHISE MODE

2 In Franchise Mode, you build your own team through the draft and then improve by developing and trading players. Team chemistry is crucial — you need to make sure your players are all happy.

BATTLE ROYALE

3 You draft a 25-man squad and then play head-to-head online, earning bonuses to further bolster your team. This is essentially an online season mode.

CONQUEST MODE

5 You need to conquer North America in Conquest Mode. You do this by taking over the territories of all 30 MLB teams, and then gambling your fan base in a series of small, quickfire baseball matches.

ONLINE

4 Sometimes all you want is a simple head-to-head. It's the pitcher vs. batter battle that really shines through.

CHECK FATIGUE

Keep an eye on your pitcher's stamina. You'll need to rotate pitchers to keep them all fresh.

EXCITE-O-METER

Take me out to the ball game.

+ Looks like real baseball
+ Hitting a homerun feels great
− Only appeals to baseball fans

STATS

460,000

You Tube views for the Flying Lap trailer.

21 circuits.

11 teams.

22 DRIVERS.

F1 2016
THE FASTEST RACING GAME AROUND

If you want authentic, then you want *F1 2016*. This simulation of one of the most technical sports in the world zeroes in on every last possible detail. Your tires degrade during the race, you need to invest in research and development during the season, you foster rivalries with other drivers, you even have to learn F1 rules concerning safety cars and formation laps. Just like the real sport, it's an incredibly demanding racing game to master. You need to invest a lot of time and energy to master *F1 2016*. It's worth it, though, because no other game has that feeling of constantly being on edge, as you try to push your car as fast as it will go while staying safe and avoiding the other cars on the track.

TIPS & TRICKS

DRIVE SAFELY
It's better to take a corner too slowly and lose position than go too fast and crash.

AVOID OTHER CARS
Collisions can lead to penalties, ruining your race, so leave plenty of room when taking corners.

TOP 5 FUN THINGS TO TRY

CAREER MODE

1 This is the meat of *F1 2016*. This mode takes place over 10 full seasons and charts your rise from fresh-faced newbie to F1 legend, with help from your team's engineers and your agent.

PLAYING AS HAAS

2 There's a unique thrill in doing well with new team Haas. Winning with either of their drivers, Romain Grosjean and Esteban Gutierrez, proves you have total mastery of *F1 2016*.

ONLINE

3 With 22-car lobbies, there's a lot of potential for carnage in *F1 2016*'s online modes. If one player is reckless, the race can become crazy!

WET RACES

5 As the rain pours down, the tracks become wet and visibility becomes poor. This is the ultimate test of your F1 skill, as you jostle for position in treacherous conditions.

TIME TRIAL

4 It's just you versus the track, as you try to set the fastest time possible. Having no other cars around completely changes your approach and means you have no excuses for slow times.

USE SLIPSTREAM
On long straights, drive directly behind cars in front to go slightly faster.

EXCITE-O-METER

Every bit as demanding as being a real F1 driver.

+ Captures every single F1 detail
+ Rewards time invested
− Very difficult to play

WHICH SPORTS GAME IS RIGHT FOR YOU?

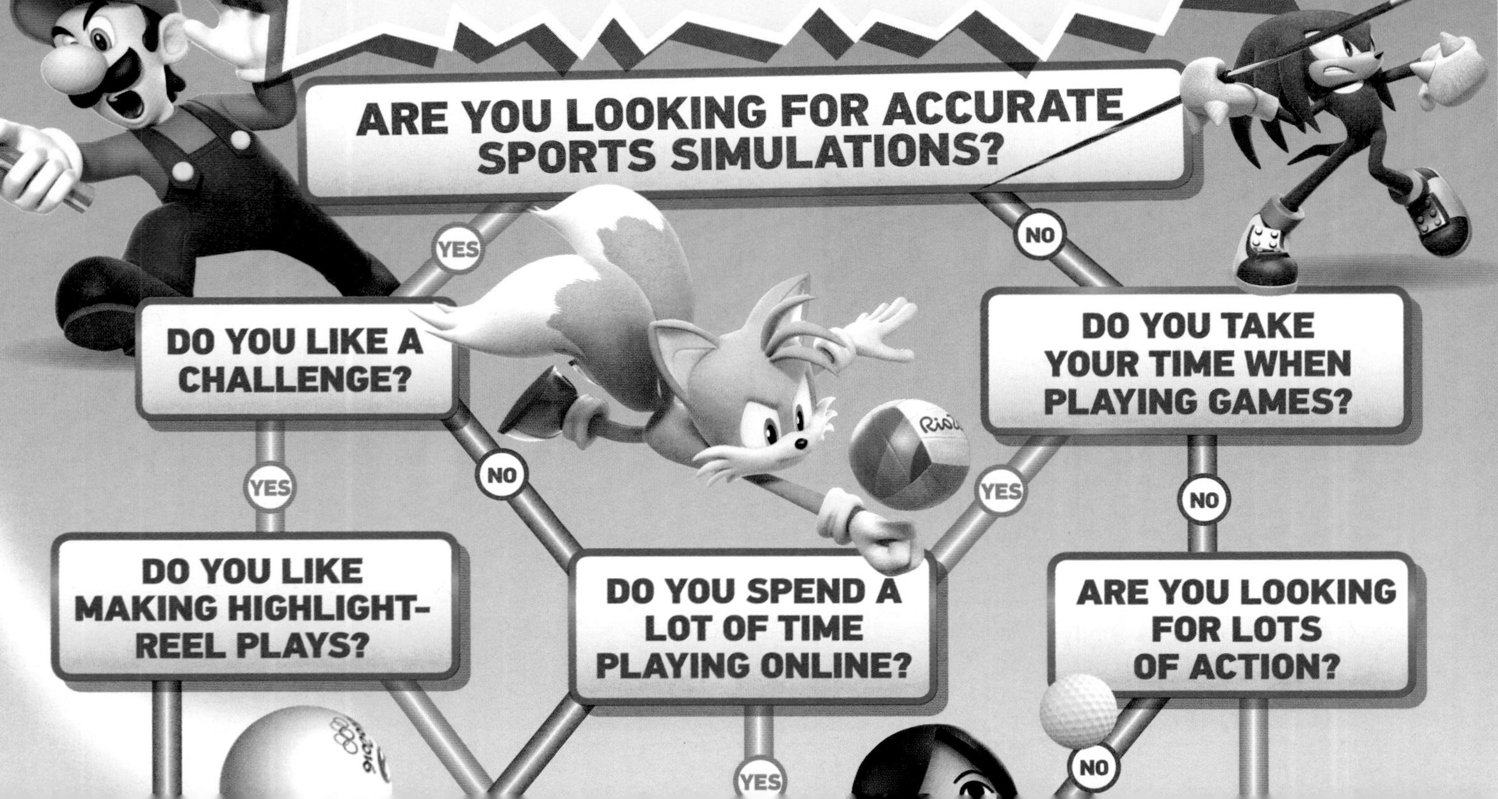

ARE YOU LOOKING FOR ACCURATE SPORTS SIMULATIONS?

DO YOU TAKE YOUR TIME WHEN PLAYING GAMES?

NO

ARE YOU LOOKING FOR LOTS OF ACTION?

NO

YES

DO YOU SPEND A LOT OF TIME PLAYING ONLINE?

YES

NO

YES

DO YOU LIKE A CHALLENGE?

DO YOU LIKE MAKING HIGHLIGHT-REEL PLAYS?

YES

DO YOU PREFER PLAYING BY YOURSELF?

YES

NO

OLLIOLLI
It's you, a skateboard, and a series of dangerous obstacles that you can trick off for high scores.

ROCKET LEAGUE
This brilliant fantasy crossover of soccer and rockets has earned millions of fans across the world, thanks to its high-speed multiplayer antics.

DO YOU MIND PLAYING MADE-UP SPORTS?

YES

NO

MADDEN
Scoring touchdowns appeals to everyone and *Madden*'s deep simulation of football is accessible and fun, no matter your skill level.

DO YOU WANT A SPORTS GAME ANYONE CAN JUST PICK UP AND PLAY?

NO

NO

YES

NO

NBA 2K
From layups in traffic to wide open three-pointers, this basketball simulation caters to every style in the sport. Dominate the game your way!

F1 2016
This sports simulation is deep, difficult, and demanding. The more time and energy you put in, the more you'll get in return.

MOST AWESOME

SPORTS GAMES

ACHIEVEMENTS & TROPHIES!

BECOME THE CHAMPION OF THE WORLD

Sports games are the ultimate in competition. Whether it's you versus your friend, the golf course, the road, or even the world, sports games demand that you conquer all obstacles in your path to become the best. But dig into the achievements or trophies list and you'll see sports games go even deeper than that. Some dare you to overcome unusual tactics, proving you're stronger than cheap coaching tricks. Some ask you to celebrate your success at turning adversity into triumph. Some even ask you to crash your car so badly that you can't race anymore. Here are some of the more interesting achievements and trophies in the world of sports games, along with how to unlock them.

ACHIEVEMENTS & TROPHIES!

F1 2016

Achievement Thanks To The Team

Purchase all upgrades for your car

COOLEST ACHIEVEMENT

DIRT RALLY

Achievement Mondays Be Like . . .

Crash your car so badly it ends your rally

The spectacular crashes in *DiRT Rally* make failure more fun than it should be. You might get this achievement without trying because *DiRT Rally* is a difficult game. But regardless, crashing is so much fun, sometimes you'll indulge in the guilty pleasure of crashing deliberately.

BE PATIENT
01 It will take roughly two seasons before you'll have enough Resource Points to acquire all the upgrades.

EARNING POINTS
02 To earn maximum points, complete all Practice Programs and Team Objectives, earn pole position, and win race.

MOST ANNOYING TROPHY

TOUR DE FRANCE 2016

Trophy Flashed

Reach 100km/h in Challenge Mode

Unlocking this achievement takes a lot of effort, determination, and some luck. The test comes from earning a gold medal for every challenge, which is needed to unlock Le Mont Blanc. This is the only track where you can reach the speed, so you need to get all those gold medals first — annoying!

DON'T SWITCH TEAMS
03 Most of all, remember to stick with your team until you get enough Resource Points. You'll lose them all if you switch!

ACHIEVEMENTS & TROPH

QUICKEST ACHIEVEMENT

NBA 2K17

🏆 **Achievement** Wait, There's More!

Celebrate after an And-1 in My CAREER/MyPARK/Pro-Am

Drive the ball to the hoop and go for a layup. If you have a quick player, you'll be fouled as you take the shot. If the shot goes in, the free throw is then known as And-1. Just push the right analog stick in any direction when the whistle blows to celebrate.

WEIRDEST TROPHY

MADDEN NFL 17

🏆 **Trophy** Antifreeze

Make a FG while iced

This achievement copies a tactic straight from the NFL, where coaches call a time-out just as the opposing kicker takes a field goal, known as icing the kicker. You need to score a field goal when a coach tries this tactic on you. You'll know you've been iced as a kicker because the field goal meter will double in size!

FUNNIEST TROPHY

DANGEROUS GOLF

🏆 **Trophy** Double Vision

Destroy a pair of Mystery Items

In a game that's about smashing everything up, this achievement requires you to . . . smash everything up! You have to seek out and destroy the mystery items for this achievement to pop, and Drop The Ball is the easiest level to do this in. You tee off between two microwaves. These are the mystery objects, so hit the ball into one microwave so it ricochets into the other.

MOST AWESOME TROPHY

NHL 17

Trophy Lifting The Cup

Win the Stanley Cup in Be A Pro mode

Be A Pro mode sees you taking control of a single player at the draft, developing him from rookie bench-warmer to superstar team captain. This achievement is awarded for lifting the ultimate prize in hockey, the Stanley Cup, with your player . . . a fitting end to any NHL career!

EASIEST ACHIEVEMENTS

PRO EVOLUTION SOCCER 2017

Achievement Super-Sub

Scoring with a substitute unlocks this achievement so put your best three strikers and midfielders on the bench, then bring them on as soon as the match begins.

RORY MCILROY PGA TOUR

Achievement Customized

All you need to do is create a custom gameplay style for this achievement to pop. Go to Gameplay Settings, dive in Custom, and change one of the settings. That's it!

DINO DINI'S KICK OFF REVIVAL

Achievement Center Score

A goal from the halfway line will do for this challenge and best of all, you can unlock it in training mode without a goalkeeper in place. A full strength shot will work.

END GAME

PES 2017

Create your own legends

It's great fun playing as the biggest teams in the world and scoring goals with superstar players. For a bigger challenge, though, try taking on the Master League mode with the original roster of low-rated players and growing the team into Champions League winners.